KAL

DRAWS
A CROWD

POLITICAL CARTOONS BY KEVIN KALLAUGHER

FOREWORD BY PAT OLIPHANT

WOODHOLME
HOUSE
PUBLISHERS

BALTIMORE, MARYLAND

Printed and bound in the
United States of America.

1 2 3 4 5
06 05 04 03 02 01 00 99 98 97

ISBN 0-9656342-6-4

Library of Congress Card Catalog
#: 97-060708

Woodholme House Publishers
1829 Reisterstown Road
Suite 130
Baltimore, Maryland 21208
Fax: (410) 653-7904
Orders: 1-800-488-0051

All the cartoons in this book are from
The Baltimore Sun, © 1992, 1993, 1994, 1995, 1996, 1997.

Kevin Kallaugher's cartoons are distributed
exclusively by Cartoonists & Writers Syndicate,
67 Riverside Drive, New York, New York, 10024.
212-362-9256 / E-MAIL: CWStoons@AOL.COM.

Cover design: Anna Marlis Burgard
Cover photograph: Jim Burger

FOREWORD

That political cartooning is indeed an art form is an idea that today eludes a great proportion of readers, editors, and, alas, many practitioners of what has been called "The Ungentlemanly Art." A large number of these people demand no more than the pointlessly exaggerated, big-noses-are-funny, comic-page approach to drawing, and the simple-minded, opinionless, malice-toward-none approach to ideas.

Political cartooning, at its best, is a confrontational art, a skillful melding of drawing, idea, and belief, carried forward on the vehicle of humorous, whimsical, or dramatic and startling artwork. It's aimed to crash headlong into the target of the moment—a kamikaze concept not well received or accepted in these timorous, politically correct closing days of the twentieth century.

If this form of expression, which depends so much on the direct involvement of its audience, should survive the current debilitation of public fervor for difficult issues, it will also have to survive the added hazards of pusillanimous editors and publishers whose only public service obligation, as they see it, is to deliver a profit to the stockholders, and to whom controversy and conflict on their pages, in the form of contentious cartoons, is total anathema.

KAL obviously accepts controversy as his daily bread, and it is quite apparent that his editors and publishers are accepting of that and even, one would imagine, valuing it. His drawing is excellent, his ideas are combative, and he spends long, careful hours developing both.

KAL's mastery of caricature—that other elusive but indispensable element, that encapsulation of the inner person—has been honed to a fine degree. The results are cause enough for optimism that this art, this strange and arcane alchemy that makes two-dimensional explosives out of simple ink and paper, will survive long into the next millennium.

This book presents for your enjoyment the work of a polished professional alchemist and kamikaze pilot who delights in what he does, and delight is another essential ingredient to the brew that is political cartooning.

What more could one ask?

Pat Oliphant
July, 1997

INTRODUCTION

I always thought that becoming a cartoonist would be difficult. I was wrong. Starting off as a cartoonist is easy. Anybody can do it. Find a joke, draw a few people, use your very best handwriting to write the caption and (presto!) you're a cartoonist!

Now try drawing another cartoon...then another. In fact, try drawing another ten thousand original cartoons. That's about how many you can expect to draw in your career. You soon discover, as I did, that becoming a cartoonist is easy—*retiring* as one is the hard part.

So here I sit, in Baltimore, at cartoon #4867 with twenty more years and over five thousand blank pieces of paper to fill. As you can guess, I'm in a never-ending and desperate quest to find new cartoon ideas.

I normally start my daily search for inspiration just after midnight. Tucked away in a studio at my home, I use the Internet to check any late-breaking news stories before I go to bed. CNN and C-Span also act as nocturnal cartoon subject advisors...and snooze inducers.

As I drift off to sleep, I find that there is a fertile moment of clarity between the time when I am conscious and comatose. A surprising number of cartoon ideas come to me then. What is not surprising is that I rarely remember any of them. A cartoonist colleague of mine, when confronted with the same dilemma, resorted to keeping a tape recorder by his bed to catalog his night's creativity. He soon dropped the idea. One morning, after he recorded what he thought was a particularly productive brainstorming session, he listened to the tape. It did not replay the pithy erudite observations he remembered recording the night before, but instead the incoherent ranting of a raving lunatic.

My radio alarm goes off at 6:50 a.m. It's tuned to the news on National Public Radio, so the first words in my ear are often "The Clinton Administration today denied any wrongdoing..." or "Another special prosecutor was appointed today...." The second words in my ear are my wife's: "Turn that thing off!"

Despite its jarring early morning attack on my senses, NPR has become an indispensable friend in the morning. Radio allows me to get on with things—shaving, ironing, preparing breakfast, browbeating the children—while still learning about the world's happenings. I share NPR with my children as I drive them to school in the morning. They, too, hold special feelings about its educational format: "Change the station and put some good music on!"

I arrive at the office and have until seven o'clock that night to come up with a cartoon for the next day's paper. The morning hours are spent reading newspapers and periodicals, talking to colleagues, answering phone calls and letters, and, in between, desparately searching for idea #4867.

The letters I get from readers range from irritated to irrational. A good eighty-five percent of the reactions I get from my cartoons are negative...and understandably so. If a reader likes what he or she sees in the newspaper they are not inclined to take the time to express their satisfaction. But if there is something in the paper that upsets them, you know you're going to hear about it. Since Baltimore has just one major newspaper, there's a good chance that every cartoon I draw is going to tick somebody off. Some of the letters I receive pose intelligent counterpoints to my cartoons. But most are agitated, emotional, and often unsigned. I get attacked for being too liberal by some and too conservative by others. Some readers take the time to send me altered versions of my cartoons with personalized, mostly obscene, embellishments. My favorite letter remains one sent to my editor. I was away on vacation and the paper used a substitute cartoonist in my spot with a caption underneath noting "KAL is on vacation." The letter writer kept it brief: "I hope KAL is enjoying his vacation as much as we are."

Politicians rarely respond directly by letter or phone to the cartoons. Sometimes I hear from aides that the politicians want original cartoons to hang in their offices. Some politicians (Al Gore and Phil Graham come to mind) keep quite a collection of cartoons. No matter how hard you might abuse these public officials in your cartoons, they want to display it on their wall. After Steve Forbes withdrew from the presidential race in 1996 he instructed the Forbes Library to purchase seventy-five cartoon originals about him. You can bet that these cartoons (including the one in this book) were less than flattering. This ability to laugh at oneself would seemingly be a necessary survival tool for those in the public spotlight.

However, there are politicians who are so sensitive to criticism that no cartoon, however innocuous, is funny to them. Former Mayor and Governor William Donald Schaefer fits into this category. He once wrote asking me, amazingly, to send him a cartoon for his personal collection. "As you charge for these depressing monstrosities, I enclose herewith the value I place upon it," His Honor wrote, and taped a penny to the letter.

As for cartoon fodder, there is no lack of material (locally, nationally, or internationally) for me to comment on. One of the unique responsibilities of the editorial cartoonist is that he or she is expected to be an expert on all things. As a result, keeping abreast of news and events happening around the world is one of the most difficult aspects of my job. As much as I might read about the news, there's always more to know.

When I watch the experts and pundits on television, I am deeply impressed by their ability to expound on a wide array of issues at a drop of a hat. I, in contrast, need time and research to come to any considered conclusions. The hours spent reading newspapers and magazines, and talking with professional colleagues, has become an essential element of the cartooning process for me. I garner as much information as I can before embarking on any chosen daily cartoon subject.

Once the research is complete, my next step is to find an unusual and provocative angle from which to portray my point of view on the subject at hand. During this time,

I do my creative thinking with a pencil and pad close by. I call this my "sketch and stretch" phase. I play around with concepts in my head and on my pad, starting with a germ of an idea adding humor, metaphors, and absurdity to stretch and tickle the idea into a fully formed cartoon. On the pad in front of me I produce little scribbles and doodles that are indecipherable to most people, but to me are visual shorthand notes of a developing cartoon.

By mid-afternoon I should have decided on a subject and contrived an angle to tackle it. I refine the cartoon carefully during the next stage—the drawing stage, which takes about four-and-a-half hours. The first two hours are spent drawing the cartoon from its preliminary sketches to a finished pencil drawing. The next two-and-a-half hours are spent applying black India ink to the pencil artwork to render it suitable for reproduction on newsprint.

As I draw, my emphasis shifts from being a journalist and commentator to being an artist. I have other considerations now—composition, caricature, and calligraphy. I make many sketches and many mistakes. But over time, out of a slew of cartoon experiments, a single drawing emerges. It's time to dedicate myself to the lonely pursuit of applying ink to the cartoon. For hours it's just me, a piece of paper, a pen, and a bottle of ink. I scratch, scratch, scratch closer to the seven o'clock deadline.

Now the drawing is finished. Well, not really finished. There's no drawing that couldn't be improved with twenty-four more hours spent working on it. So the drawing merely stops. I escort it down to the composing room to be scanned for the next day's paper. When I look at it, I see nothing but the mistakes I made and the lessons I could learn for my next cartoon.

It's time to head home. It's getting dark. On the way, in my car, my old friend NPR talks to me: "The Clinton Administration today denied any wrongdoing...." I look at my watch. It's 7:30. I've just finished work and already it's time to start again—time to start working on cartoon #4868.

Kevin Kallaugher

THE NEW SHOW IN TOWN

Think back to 1992. Twelve years of Republican rule was about to end. The nation was poised to elect, reluctantly, its first Baby-Boomer President. Congress and the Presidency were firmly in the hands of the Democrats. The specter of change nurtured great dreams for some, nightmares for others. From the moment Bill and Hillary arrived in the White House, Washington was a changed place. A place full of hope, optimism, and abundance...for editorial cartoonists.

After two terms of
Ronald Reagan and one
of George Bush, the nation
was ready to try the
Democrats on for size.
(unpublished)
November 3, 1992

TO THE
VICTOR
GOES
THE
SPOILS

A jubilant Clinton got a taste
of challenges to come.

November 4, 1992

Despite a narrow victory,
the President thought he
had been given a mandate
to overhaul the nation's
troubled health care system.

December 6, 1992

Americans were concerned with cutbacks in services...

January 22, 1992

...but were also demanding cutbacks in rising medical costs.

October 31, 1993

A secretive health care task force headed by First Lady Hillary Clinton endorsed wide-ranging changes. Critics immediately painted the task force's calls for an enlarged government bureaucracy as "socialized medicine."

September 29, 1993

Deemed cumbersome
and over ambitious,
the President's grand plans
for the nation's health care
(and his popularity rating)
took a plunge.

August 3, 1994

Bill Clinton, former draft dodger now Commander-in-Chief, was scrutinized closely by the military.

April 1, 1993

With the Cold War over, the Pentagon found itself fighting more complex internal problems.

January 27, 1993

An inept and indecisive Clinton stumbled through his first six months in office.

July 21, 1993

A steady trickle of stories relating to a failed real estate venture in Arkansas darkened the President's days…

March 6, 1994

WHITEWATER HEARINGS

…and brightened the Republicans'.

March 20, 1994

The fallout from the Whitewater scandal tarred Clinton's friends, family, and policymaking.

March 16, 1994

Smarting from her disasterous foray into health care reform, the First Lady retreated from the public spotlight. However, revelations from her past, including that she had made a bundle on cattle futures under questionble circumstances, returned her to center stage.

March 31, 1994

Files taken from the office of Vince Foster after his death mysteriously disappeared from the White House. Meanwhile, numerous confidential personal FBI files of prominent politicians mysteriously appeared *in* the White House.

June 30, 1996

HEADING
IN A NEW
DIRECTION

MORE CUTS

BUDGET

MORE SPENDING

KAL '94
BALTO. SUN

The President tried to cobble
together an economic policy.

February 9, 1994

One thing for sure,
he could always depend
on support from Capitol Hill.

June 27, 1993

When the economy galloped off, the President's popularity pulled up lame.

October 6, 1994

Clinton's low rating hurt the Democrats in the 1994 mid-term elections. The Republicans soundly trounced the opponents and dreamt of dominance.

November 16, 1994

Newt Gingrich became the
first Republican Speaker of
the House in forty years.
"Newt" became a household
name and a symbol
of change...

April 7, 1995

...much to the chagrin of the Democrats—and some Republicans.

November 14, 1994

Newt and his cohorts
attacked many of
Washington's sacred cows…

January 20, 1995

...and sacred mammoths.

September 20, 1995

HAMMERING
OUT THEIR
DIFFERENCES

KAL 92
BALTO. SUN
CW SYND.

GOP

PRO LIFE!

PRO CHOICE

The Republicans tried and failed to fudge their stand on abortion.

August 12, 1992

The new budget reflected
Republican priorities.

May 13, 1995

His early left-wing policies rebuffed, the President set out to reinvent himself as a moderate to help gain re-election in 1996.

January 26, 1995

ELECTION FOLLIES

They were tied one match a piece. The Democrats won big in 1992; the Republicans bounced back in '94. The 1996 election promised to be the deciding bout, crowning once and for all the undisputed champion in Washington. The GOP carried the momentum, but were fading fast. Bill Clinton, "The Comeback Kid," reinvented himself for the 457th time. Ross Perot, to the deafening applause of car-toonists around the country, entered the fray, setting the stage for a classic three-way battle. When they eyed the stature of their three candidates as they entered the ring, the voters became poised and ready. They anxiously sat on the edge of their seats, poised and ready…to leave the arena.

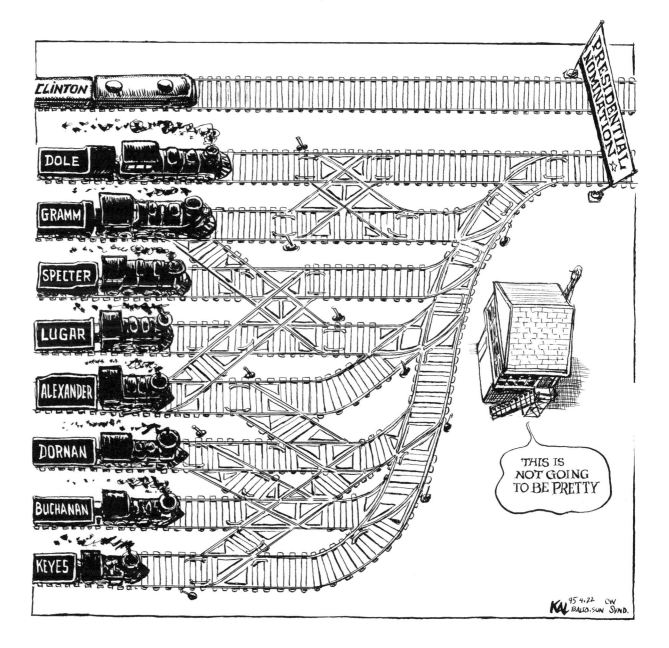

The Republicans thought that a weak Clinton would be easy to derail.

April 22, 1995

The current crop of presidential contenders failed to inspire the American public. Desperate, both parties courted Gulf War hero Colin Powell to be on their presidential ticket. After much deliberation, Powell proved himself to be both a Republican and singularly uninterested in high office.

October 1, 1993

A strong showing by millionaire Steve Forbes and arch-conservative Pat Buchanan in the New Hampshire Republican primary spelled trouble for front-runner Bob Dole.

January 6, 1996

Republican voters looked in vain for a formidable challenger to Bill Clinton.

February 29, 1996

Dole eventually
overwhelmed a weak
GOP field only to face
new challenges.

March 26, 1996

Ross Perot decided to have his own party. Everyone was invited, but no one showed up.

August 13, 1995

Political soundbites dominated the airwaves.

November 2, 1994

Clinton's campaign strategy was to win over the predominantly female "swing voter."

October 29, 1996

The difference between
the two presidential
candidates was more of style
than of substance.

May 22, 1996

Down in the polls,
a desperate Bob Dole
decided to "go negative"
and focus his campaign on
the President's numerous
character flaws.

October 17, 1996

One week before the November election, revelations of unscrupulous campaign money raising practices by the Democrats rocked the White House. The subsequent voter fallout wasn't enough to cost Clinton the election, but squashed any hopes of the Democrats recapturing the House and the Senate.

November 3, 1996

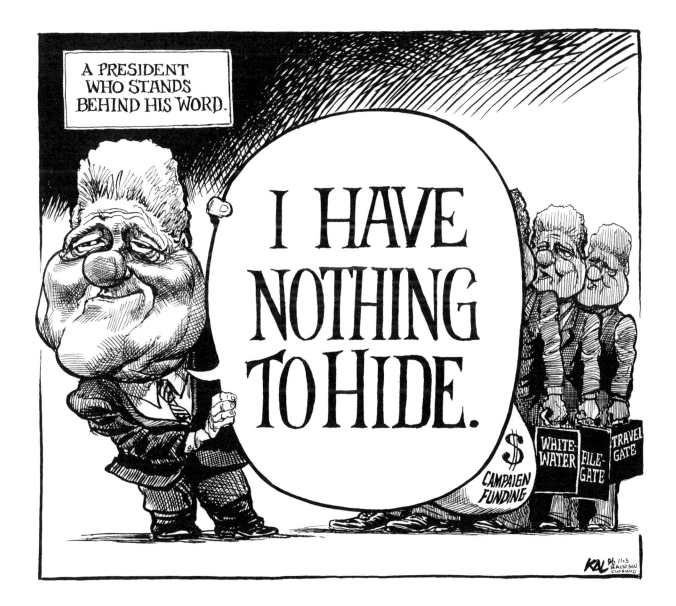

House Speaker Newt Gingrich faced ethical troubles of his own. When questioned whether a college course he was teaching was really an illegal fund-raising tool, the Speaker was economical with the truth.

January 7, 1997

The House ethics
committee ruled on the case.
Gingrich was rebuked,
but not reassigned.

January 23, 1997

Questionable Democratic fund-raising activities also befell the White House. This time suspicion centered on use of the Lincoln Bedroom and intimate "coffee klatches" with the President.

February 27, 1997

Both parties paid lip service to campaign finance reform.

March 11, 1997

President Clinton, famous for his waffling, remained consistent in one area—scandal.

February 20, 1997

Despite Congressional hearings on the subject, the influence of "big money" on America's election process carried on.

February 18, 1997

Clinton and the Republicans were virtually indistinguishable in the 1997 budget negotiations.

May 10, 1997

Even five years into the Clinton Administration, some questions on Whitewater remained unresolved.

June 22, 1997

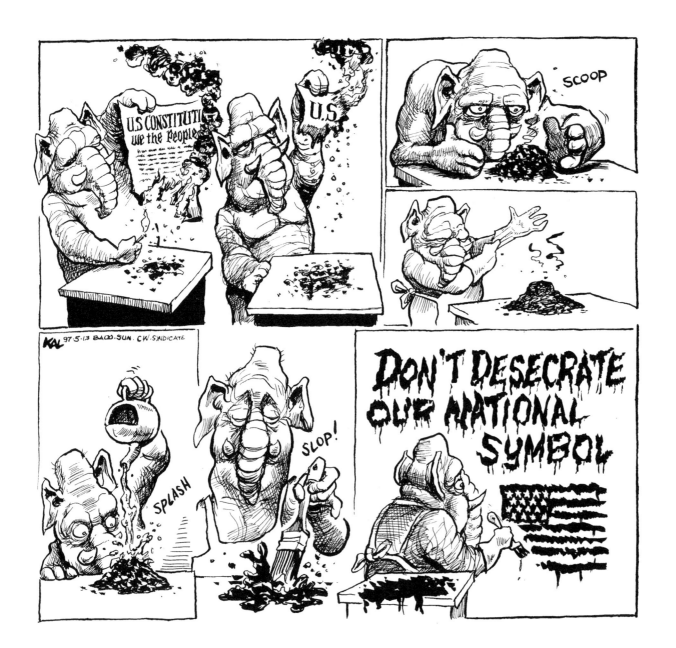

The Republicans edged closer to realizing their dream of a constitutional amendment outlawing flag burning.

May 13, 1997

Paula Jones returned to the headlines when the Supreme Court allowed her sexual harassment case against Bill Clinton to proceed.

May 29, 1997

With an approval rating of over 60%, President Bill Clinton was setting an example to the nation.

January 30, 1997

THE WORLD STAGE

The post-Cold War world presented complex and unpredictable problems that stumped even the most experienced foreign diplomat. George Bush, as qualified as anyone to meet these challenges, lost the '92 election, in part because he was considered too much of a foreign policy president.

Enter Bill Clinton. The most powerful nation in the world now boasted a leader whose idea of a "foreign dilemma" was which Chinese restaurant to frequent, and whose idea of "foreign affairs" involved dating someone from outside Little Rock, Arkansas.

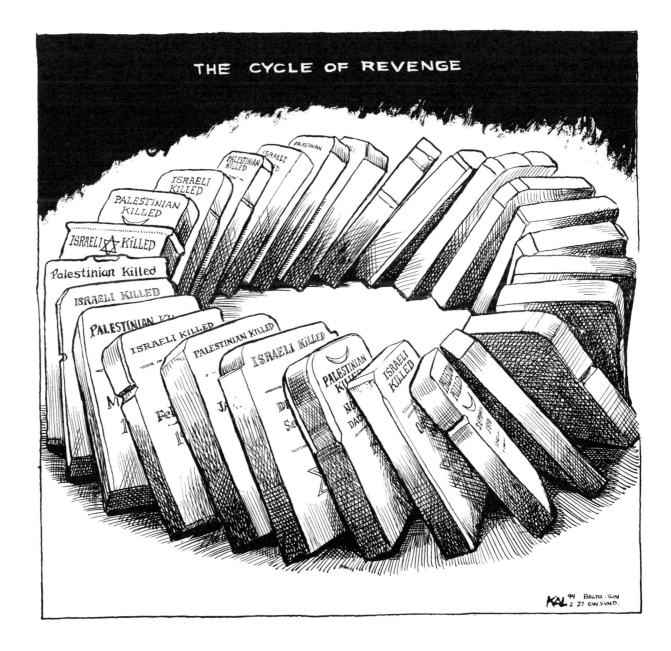

THE CYCLE OF REVENGE

The Arab-Israeli conflict seemed to be on a downward spiral.

February 27, 1994

But a move by Yasser Arafat and the Palestine Liberation Organization to "recognize" the existance of the state of Israel reenergized the moribund peace process.

September 1, 1993

Israeli and Palestinian
leaders met in Norway to
hammer out their differences.
The historic "Oslo Accords"
emerged, establishing
a framework for
peaceful coexistence.

September 12, 1993

THE HANDSHAKE
PHASE TWO

KAL 94 1-4 CWS.
BALTO.SUN

In a famous ceremony at the White House, Israeli Prime Minister Yitzak Rabin and PLO leader Yasser Arafat shook hands. In the weeks and months to follow old contentions resurfaced.

January 4, 1994

The assassination of Yitzak Rabin at the hands of an Israeli extremist saddened the world, and jeopardized an already tenuous peace process.

November 12, 1995

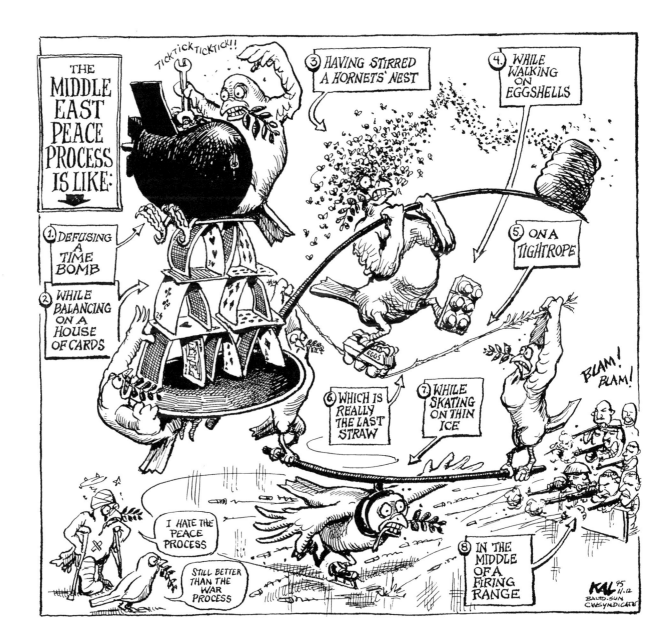

Israel and the PLO turned
to America for help.

May 2, 1996

Russia, desperately strapped for cash, looked to earn money by exporting nuclear expertise to its neighbors to the south.

April 13, 1995

Despite many adversities, Russian President Boris Yeltsin tenuously held onto power.

January 13, 1994

He battled crime in Moscow, rebels in Chechnya, and nationalists in Parliament. Still, he managed to be re-elected in a robust western-style campaign only to wind up hospitalized with a heart condition.

July 14, 1996

President Clinton thought the best way to stabilize Europe was to bolster and expand NATO... much to the dismay of Russia.

February 22, 1997

The breakup of the former Yugoslavia posed a complex challenge to the transatlantic alliance.

April 12, 1993

Graphic news reports of the systematic murder of thousands of Bosnian citizens shocked the world. Former President Jimmy Carter, developing a new career as a negotiator, stepped into the picture. After numerous diplomatic initiatives failed to stem the "ethnic cleansing," swift military action by NATO forces forged a temporary peace.

December 16, 1994

Madeleine Albright, the first female Secretary of State, favored a more assertive foreign policy than her predecessor.

January 12, 1997

The President wanted to put more emphasis on achievements in foreign affairs during his second term.

December 8, 1996

When it came to the world stage, Clinton needed all the help his foreign policy team could provide.

September 8, 1994

Various troubles plagued the world's elite nations...and we thought things were bad in the United States.

July 8, 1994

While Japanese goods were commonplace in the United States, American products were less welcome in Japan.

February 17, 1994

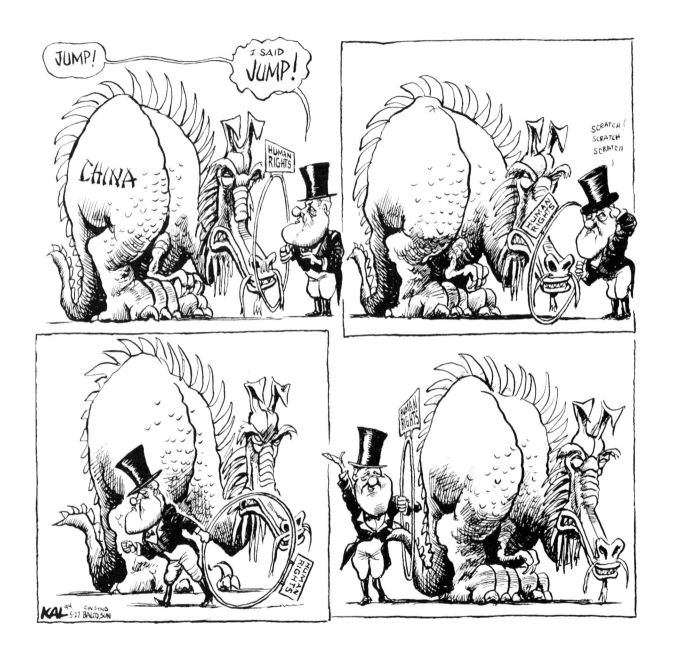

With Russia diminished as a superpower, the U.S. regarded the prosperous and repressive China as a likely future challenger.

May 27, 1994

Chinese diplomacy pitted the Far East against the mid-west.

May 21, 1996

The United Nations tried to expand its role as a diplomatic and military force in the world…

June 30, 1992

...with mixed results.

June 24, 1993

In a peaceful transfer
of power, Nelson Mandela
became the first black
president in South Africa's
history.

May 3, 1994

Like many African
nations, Zaire, now the
Congo, suffered at the
hands of its leaders.

May 8, 1997

After seventeen years
of Conservative rule,
Britain elected a new,
more centrist Labour Party.

May 3, 1997

Change visited Britain's royalty, too. What seemed like a fairytale ended in 1996 when Prince Charles and Princess Diana divorced. Tragically, the princess died in a car accident in August, 1997.

December 4, 1992

When you're the only
superpower it's lonely
at the top…or the bottom.

December 12, 1996

GENERAL MAYHEM

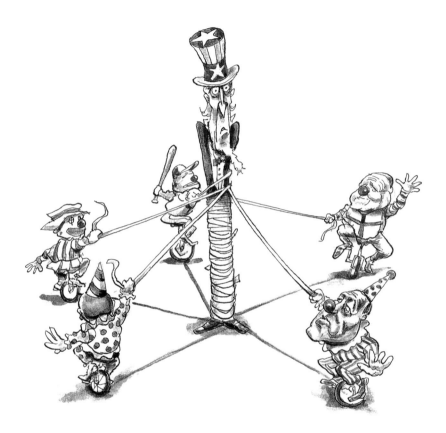

Tony Auth, political cartoonist for the *Philadelphia Inquirer*, said to me upon my return to the United States in 1988, "You're going to love working in this country...there are so many problems." Sad but true, cartoonists do thrive to some degree on pandemonium to keep themselves in business. Thankfully for us cartoonists, the United States is the world leader for creating (and some people say exporting) chaos. This section is dedicated to all the misfits, maniacs, and lunatics who make this great country what it is today...nuts.

The murder trial of former Heisman Trophy-winner and movie actor O.J. Simpson mesmerized the country.

September 27, 1994

Judge Ito's courtroom didn't
inspire confidence.

August 18, 1995

The media gorged the country's enormous appetite for all things O.J.

March 24, 1995

The marathon made-for-TV trial upstaged more important stories.

February 6, 1997

With two verdicts—innocent in criminal court and guilty in civil court—everyone had something to hate about the O.J. trials.

October 4, 1995

People weren't sure
if cloning was a real
advancement of science.

February 25, 1997

The Hubble Telescope, the Pathfinder space probe, the comet Hale-Bopp, and the "X-Files" all peaked our natural curiosity for outer space.

August 8, 1996

Meanwhile, the search for intelligent life on television pressed on.

May 24, 1994

New rating labels
for television pleased
some parents.

December 28, 1996

But a method of policing a new medium proved to be more elusive.

March 19, 1997

The World Wide Web promised wealth and opportunity—to those who could afford a computer.

June 19, 1997

In America's hinterlands, the once laughable paranoid "militias" became a dangerous force.

April 28, 1995

The murder of children and civilians by a terrorist bomb in Oklahoma City brought America face to face with an unfamiliar demon.

April 20, 1995

In sharp contrast to the
O.J. Simpson debacle,
the trial and subsequent
sentencing of bombing
suspect Timothy McVeigh
was disciplined and sober.

June 3, 1997

Across the country, "religious" terrorists targeted abortion clinics.

January 18, 1997

The capture of the "Unabomber" suspect and the FBI seige of the "Freemen" militia group focused the country's attention on Montana.

April 14, 1996

America's national parks became overcrowded and underfunded.

September 1, 1996

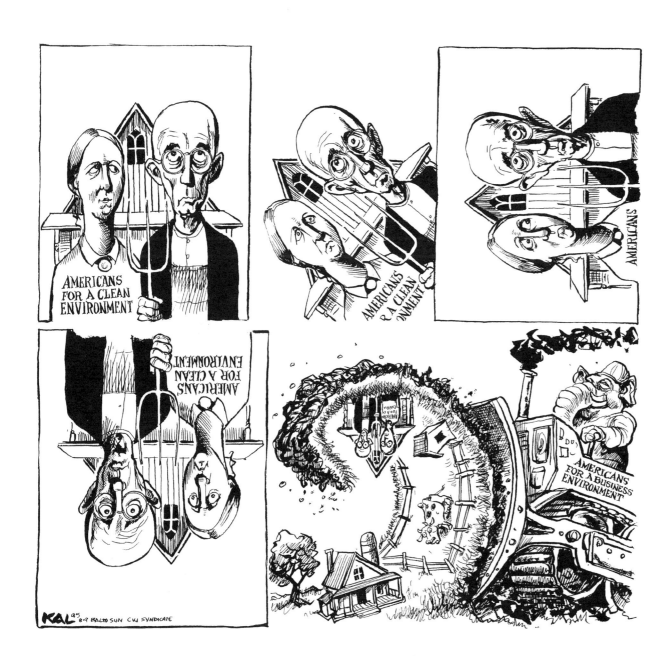

The Republicans wanted to roll back popular environmental legislation.

August 9, 1995

Big business made
concerted efforts to water
down the Clean Water Act.

May 20, 1995

After decades of lying about the dangerous effects of cigarettes, a very health-conscious and litigious America eventually punished the rich tobacco companies.

May 18, 1997

If only the planet would
stop "smoking" so much.

March 30, 1995

Hunger
is not a
Foreign
word...

WORLD HUNGER

U.S. UNDER-FED

Despite a robust economy,
the gap between the rich and
the poor in the United States
grew rapidly in the '90s.

August 24, 1996

The federal government
vainly hoped that its cuts
in social spending would
be offset by increased
intervention by charities
and businesses.

April 16, 1997

We're a company of the Nineties, Woodson. We demand complete and utter loyalty and we will return that very same loyalty right up to the day that we fire you.

In the '90s, "downsizing" and "restructuring" became new euphemisms for a familiar dilemma.

June 8, 1996

The Stock Market's upward antics defied all reasoning. In July 1997, it broke the 8,000-point plateau.

April 24, 1997

Across America, state legislatures and Indian reservations believed gambling would deliver them to fiscal nirvana.

November 4, 1995

A series of sexual harassment scandals from Tailhook to Aberdeen Proving Ground left the military scrambling for explanations.

November 1996

Pope John Paul II travelled
the world spreading the
Church's message…

August 18, 1993

...but not everyone
was listening.

December 20, 1992

The United States
continued its love affair
with the bullet…

April, 1993

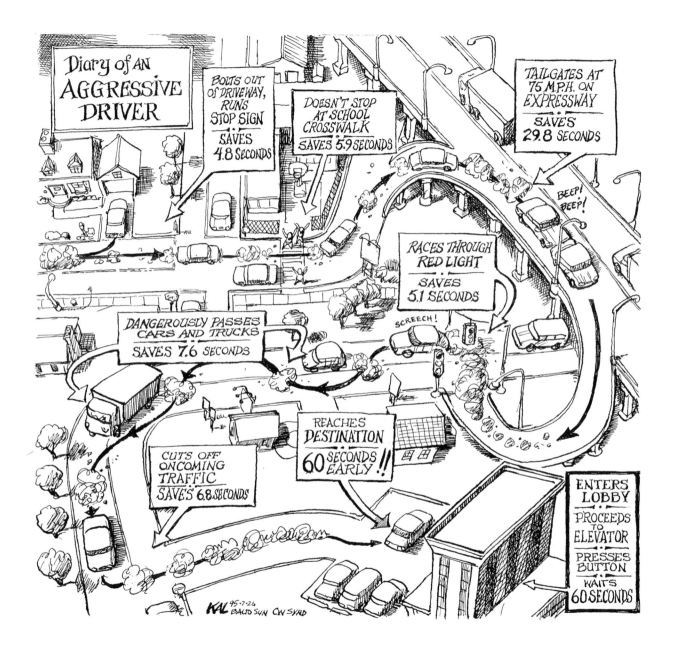

...and its love affair with an another dangerous weapon.

July 26, 1996

Professional sports salaries, and ticket prices, went through the roof.

June 15, 1997

Sports figures as role models seemed to be a thing of the past.

April 12, 1997

Some states, led by California, set out to dismantle age old Affirmatve Action programs.

July 2, 1996

Supreme Court Justice
Thurgood Marshall
left an enduring mark.

January 26, 1993

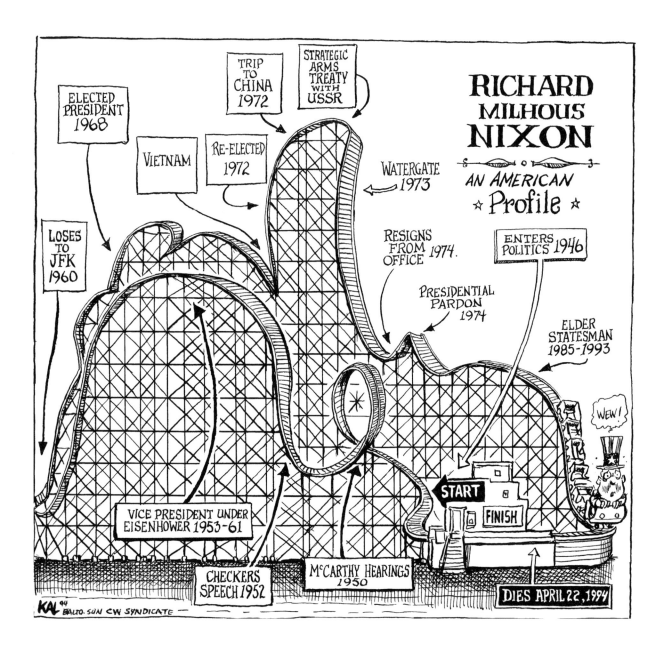

Meanwhile,
President Richard Nixon's
legacy was more of a
question mark.

April 23, 1994

President Bill Clinton is leaving an ample legacy of both fact and fiction for the history books.

January 28, 1992

Getting kids to read those history books is another thing altogether.

September 6, 1994

MADCAP MARYLAND

There is an unwritten rule in journalism suggesting that the farther a news story is from the paper's hometown, the more sensational the story has to be in order to make it in the paper. A comparison of sorts then can be made: the shenanigans of Baltimore's aggressive drivers equals a subway fire in New York equals a towering inferno in Los Angeles equals a tsunami flooding Japan, etc. Not that Baltimoreans are not concerned about subways, infernos, and tsunamis, but it's only natural that people are more sensitive to issues that take place on their doorsteps (or, in Baltimore's case, on their stoops).

Because of this natural tendency, drawing cartoons on local issues is the most fun of all. The cartoons are read and analyzed by the very subjects lampooned. The citizenry react with elation and irritation. In some rare cases, the cartoon may actually change things for the better.

This final section is dedicated to the notion that all politics is local, or to be more accurate, all politics is *loco*.

Baltimore Mayor Kurt Schmoke made many fruitless attempts to thwart the decline in the city's school system.

March 10, 1996

The mayor wasn't
the only one responsible
for the decline.

June 24, 1994

In a landmark decision, the City of Baltimore ceded some governing authority for the city schools to the State of Maryland in exchange for millions in additional funds.

November 14, 1996

An overzealous policy
of demolishing vacant city
houses created more
problems than it solved.

April 8, 1997

Housing Commissioner Daniel Henson used a combative, confrontional demeanor to offset criticism of housing department policies.

February 24, 1996

Kurt Schmoke was faced in the Democratic mayoral primary by City Council President Mary Pat Clarke. Even former Governor and Mayor Schaefer snarled about coming out of retirement. Schmoke easily withstood the challenge and returned to office for a third term.

August 21, 1995

As in so many parts of America, death by handgun became commonplace in Baltimore.

January 3, 1993

Even the most modest efforts at gun control met opposition.

November 19, 1995

The Baltimore Police Department appointed a new Commissioner and saw some improvement in crime statistics, but still faced monumental challenges.

August 6, 1993

The State Police's raid
on Baltimore's infamous
"Block" was big on show
but low on results.

March 16, 1994

Like other underfunded jurisdictions around the country, Baltimore entertained the get-rich-quick dreams of casinos.

April 28, 1996

Similarly, Governor William Donald Schaefer embraced Keno as a way to boost state coffers.

January 31, 1993

Perhaps Keno was a step toward bigger things.

December 13, 1994

The rich gambling interests lobbied heavily in Annapolis to woo the undecided.

October 3, 1995

Mayor Schmoke set out to save the floundering $150 million Baltimore Convention Center. His plan to build a subsidized "Convention Center" hotel hit a snag when the site he chose was no closer than a mile away.

July 3, 1997

The 1994 election produced one of the nation's closest ever gubernatorial races.

November 10, 1994

Democrat Parris Glendening
squeaked by, but
Republican Ellen Sauerbrey
challenged the results.

November 16, 1994

She earned herself the nickname "Ellen Sourgrapes."

January 10, 1994

Parris Glendening,
a college professor, had a lot
to learn about governing.

January 16, 1996

Decades of suburban sprawl threatened to turn Maryland's green fields into concrete jungles.

September 21, 1995

For many,
Governor Glendening
redeemed himself by taking
a popular stand
against overcrowding.

February 1, 1997

Glendening's lack of communication skills made him unpopular with legislators in Annapolis.

January 9, 1997

The 1998 gubernatorial
race started early.

April 6, 1997

April marks a Baltimore ritual: out of the winter doldrums and into the spring dugouts.

April 5, 1994

Escalating salaries, ticket prices, and concessions pushed fans to the limit.

April 26, 1994

To the pride of Oriole fans, the 1993 Baseball All-Star game was played at Baltimore's new Camden Yards stadium.

July 13, 1993

Baseball players and owners argued over money (what else?). A prolonged strike ensued with the losers being...(who else?). The dispute cancelled the 1994 World Series.

April 4, 1995

Cal Ripken's astonishing consecutive game streak set records and restored some class to a tarnished sport.

September 6, 1996

Still greiving over the theft of their beloved Colts, Baltimore desperately searched and eventually stole an NFL franchise from Cleveland. Baltimore's short-lived CFL Stallions galloped off to Montreal.

November 5, 1995

The Cleveland Browns became the Baltimore Ravens and the taxpayers became concerned.

November 14, 1995

No sooner had Maryland landed its first NFL team in a decade, then Governor Glendening enticed a second team, the Washington Redskins, to move to Laurel in Prince George's County.

December 5, 1995

The Governor tried to sell his plan to heated taxpayers.

February 1, 1996

The Ravens' millionaire owner Art Modell pleaded poverty to the state legislators and eventually received generous financial breaks.

February 11, 1996

Any pretenses that
Baltimore was a "big player"
in the country's business
community suffered a blow
when a high-profile
institution and stalwart
firm merged with outsiders.

April 10, 1997

The Pope made an historic
visit to Charm City.

October 8, 1995

Baltimoreans longed for a break from the incessant and record-setting cold of the winter of '96.

January 9, 1996

Memories of the chill soon melted away when the summer of '97 rolled around.

May 1, 1997

Maryland became the first state in the nation to require area codes for local calls, forcing dialers to punch ten digits even if just phoning a neighbor.

May 1, 1997

The remaining residents of Baltimore celebrated the city's bicentennial with hope....hope that it will celebrate its tricentennial.

March 22, 1997

ABOUT
THE CARTOONIST

Kevin Kallaugher (KAL) draws political cartoons for *The Baltimore Sun* and *The Economist*. He started his career in 1978 in London, England, when *The Economist* discovered him and made him the magazine's first resident cartoonist in its 145-year history.

A Harvard graduate who spent ten years in England, Kevin returned to the United States in 1988 to join *The Sun*. The native of Connecticut now resides in the Baltimore area with his wife and two children.

His cartoons have appeared in *The Observer, The Sunday Telegraph, International Herald Tribune, Le Monde, Der Spiegel, Pravda, Daily Yomiuri, The New York Times, Time,* *Newsweek, The Washington Post,* and *U.S. News and World Report,* among many other distinguished publications.

Past President of the Association of American Editorial Cartoonists, Kevin has had many one-man exhibitions in London, New York, Washington, and Baltimore. His many honors include Italy's Grafica Internazionale Award, the Witty World International Cartoon Festival's Best Editorial Cartoon Award, and the Cartoonist Club of Great Britain's Feature Cartoonist of the Year Award.

KAL Draws a Crowd is Kevin's third book, following *Drawn from the Economist* (1988) and *KALtoons* (1992).

ACKNOWLEDGMENTS

The cartoonist and author thanks the publisher and editors of *The Baltimore Sun* for editorial support over the years. Particularly, thanks to Joe Sterne, who brought KAL back to America from England in 1988 and who served as a valuable mentor until his retirement in 1997; Jim Preston and Jim Burger for their help with the cover illustration; and Cliff Janney for his help in preparing the artwork for publication. Finally, the author thanks Gregg Wilhelm and Anna Burgard for their patience and good humor during this book-making adventure.